# SUPER SCIENCE FEATS:
## MEDICAL BREAKTHROUGHS
# ANTIBIOTICS

by Alicia Z. Klepeis

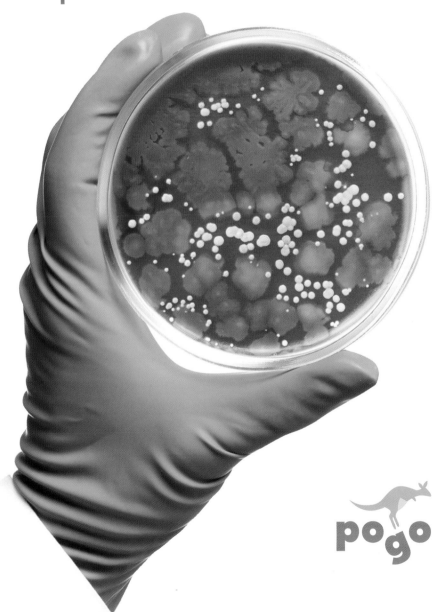

pogo

# Ideas for Parents and Teachers

Pogo Books let children practice reading informational text while introducing them to nonfiction features such as headings, labels, sidebars, maps, and diagrams, as well as a table of contents, glossary, and index.

Carefully leveled text with a strong photo match offers early fluent readers the support they need to succeed.

## Before Reading

- "Walk" through the book and point out the various nonfiction features. Ask the student what purpose each feature serves.
- Look at the glossary together. Read and discuss the words.

## Read the Book

- Have the child read the book independently.
- Invite him or her to list questions that arise from reading.

## After Reading

- Discuss the child's questions. Talk about how he or she might find answers to those questions.
- Prompt the child to think more. Ask: Did you know what antibiotics were before reading this book? What more would you like to learn about them?

Pogo Books are published by Jump!
5357 Penn Avenue South
Minneapolis, MN 55419
www.jumplibrary.com

Library of Congress Cataloging-in-Publication Data

Names: Klepeis, Alicia, 1971- author.
Title: Antibiotics / by Alicia Z. Klepeis.
Description: Minneapolis: Jump!, Inc., [2021]
Series: Super science feats: medical breakthroughs
Includes index. | Audience: Ages 7-10
Identifiers: LCCN 2020025860 (print)
LCCN 2020025861 (ebook)
ISBN 9781645277958 (hardcover)
ISBN 9781645277965 (paperback)
ISBN 9781645277972 (ebook)
Subjects: LCSH: Antibiotics–Juvenile literature.
Bacteria–Effect of drugs on–Juvenile literature.
Medicine–History–Juvenile literature.
Classification: LCC RM267 .K597 2021 (print)
LCC RM267 (ebook) | DDC 615.7/92–dc23
LC record available at https://lccn.loc.gov/2020025860
LC ebook record available at https://lccn.loc.gov/2020025861

Editor: Eliza Leahy
Designer: Michelle Sonnek

Photo Credits: grebcha/Shutterstock, cover (left), 1; goir/Shutterstock, cover (right); Guzel Studio/Shutterstock, 3; Peter Purdy/Getty, 4; zmeel/iStock, 5; Olha Rohulya/Shutterstock, 6-7; Al Fenn/Getty, 8-9 (foreground); Anelina/Shutterstock, 8-9 (background); tab1962/iStock, 10-11; Andrey_Popov/Shutterstock, 12; Kateryna Kon/Shutterstock, 13; Dr. Kari Lounatmaa/Science Source, 14-15 (bacteria cell); Shutterstock, 14-15 (background); lunopark/Shutterstock, 16-17; unoL/Shutterstock, 18; aslysun/Shutterstock, 19; andresr/iStock, 20-21; Protasov AN/Shutterstock, 23.

Printed in the United States of America at Corporate Graphics in North Mankato, Minnesota.

# TABLE OF CONTENTS

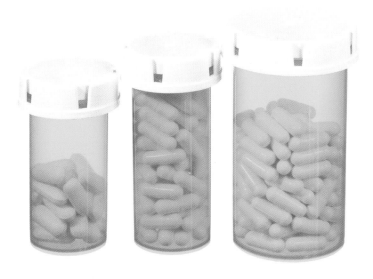

# CHAPTER 1

# FROM MOLD TO MEDICINE

The year was 1928. Alexander Fleming was a scientist. He studied **bacteria**. They were the kind that made people sick.

Alexander Fleming

bacteria

Something odd happened while he was away from his lab. Some bacteria died. But how? What had killed them?

The answer was **mold**. It was the kind that made **penicillin**. Fleming studied it. Other scientists did, too. What did they find? It could kill bacteria that caused **infections**.

This was huge news! Why? Until this time, many infections caused by bacteria could not be **cured**. They were often deadly.

**DID YOU KNOW?**

Bacteria are tiny. Millions can fit on the tip of a pen. Billions live in your body. Most help you. How? They help your body break down food.

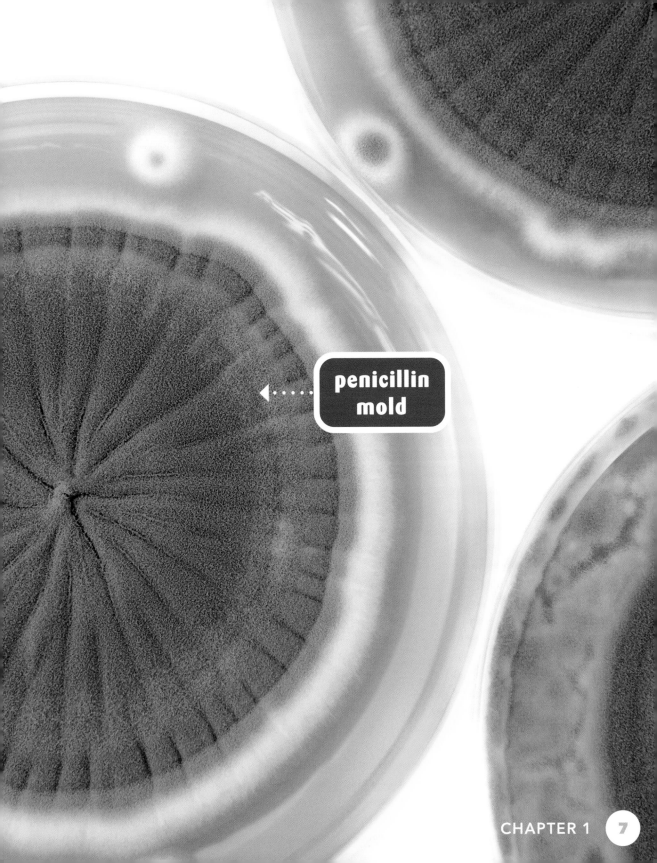

penicillin mold

Penicillin was the first **antibiotic**. In the 1940s, doctors began using it widely. How? They gave people shots. It cured infections. It healed wounds. It saved many lives.

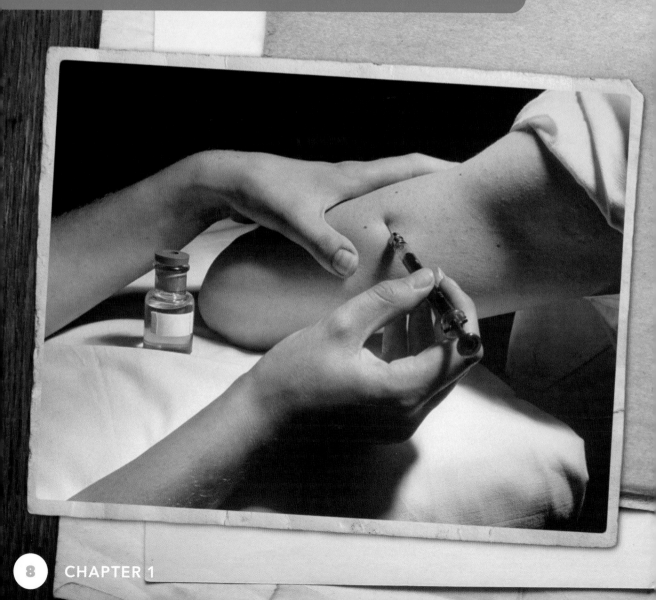

# TAKE A LOOK!

How was penicillin made? Take a look!

 1. Mold grew. It was collected.

 2. Sugar was added. Other ingredients were added, too. The mold grew faster.

3. The mold and penicillin were separated.

 4. The penicillin was **refined**. It was put into bottles.

pill ·····▶

Scientists wanted to find other antibiotics. Did they? Yes! Now there are more than 100!

We still use penicillin. People still get shots. But now it also comes in other forms such as pills.

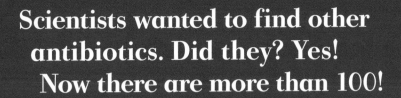

## DID YOU KNOW?

There are many forms of antibiotics. Like what? One is liquid. You drink it. Drops are another. They work on eye and ear infections. Sprays and lotions are two more. These work on cuts. Gels work on cuts, too.

# CHAPTER 2

# HOW THEY WORK

Have you had strep throat? This is an infection. Bacteria cause it. How? First, they enter the body. One way is through cuts in the skin. Another way is through the nose or mouth.

In the body, bacteria act fast. They multiply. Your body may need help fighting them. A doctor might give you an antibiotic.

bacteria

bacteria
cell

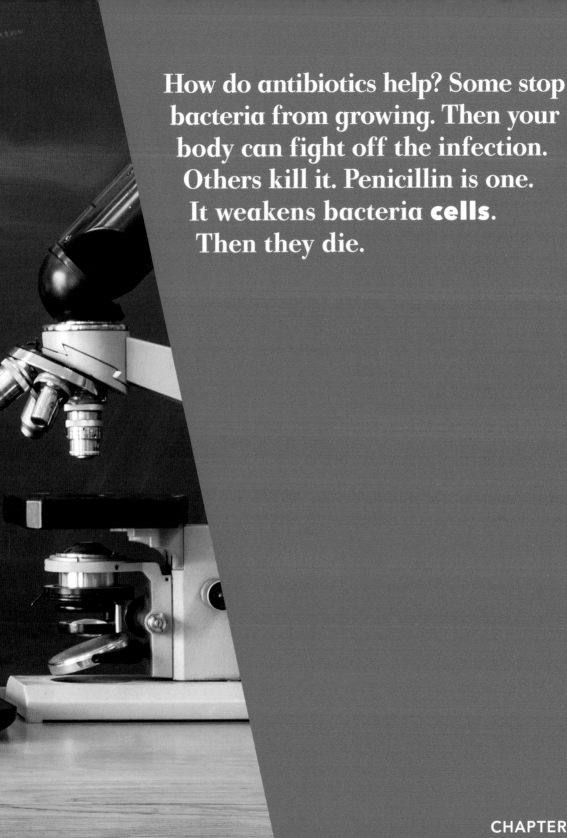

How do antibiotics help? Some stop bacteria from growing. Then your body can fight off the infection. Others kill it. Penicillin is one. It weakens bacteria **cells**. Then they die.

Antibiotics do not treat all infections. Why? They only work against bacteria. They do not kill infections caused by **viruses**. One example is COVID-19. Another is the flu.

There are other ways to fight viruses. How? One way is **vaccines**.

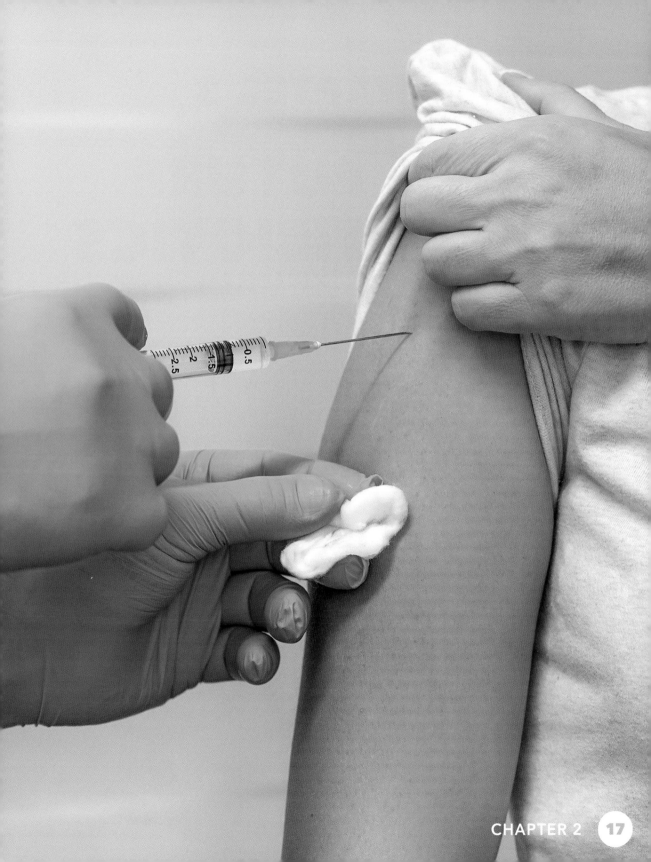

# CHAPTER 3

# THE FUTURE OF ANTIBIOTICS

Bacteria can change. They can become **resistant** to antibiotics. What does that mean? Antibiotics do not work. They cannot kill the cells. They cannot stop them from growing.

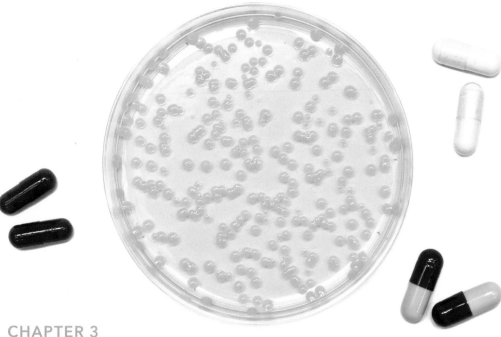

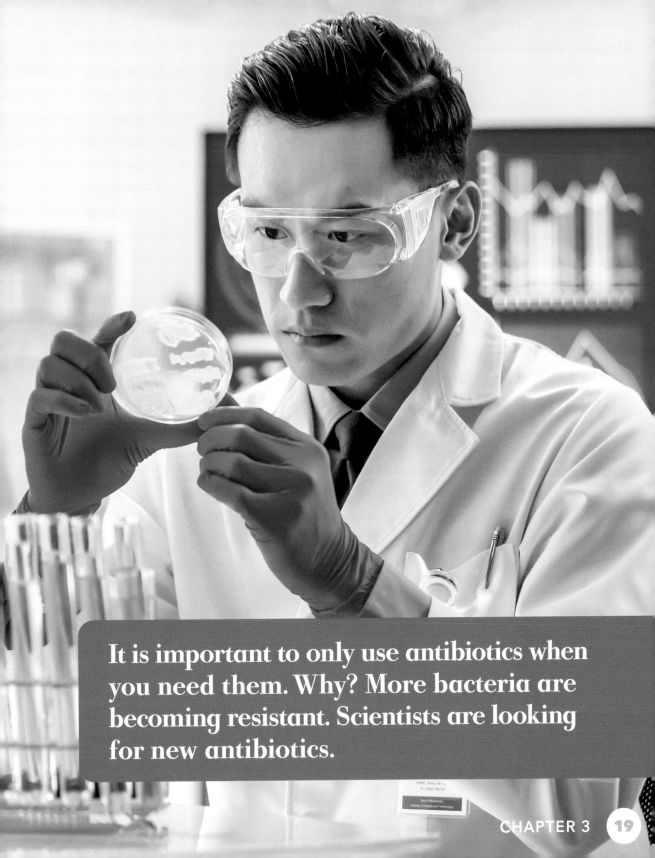

It is important to only use antibiotics when you need them. Why? More bacteria are becoming resistant. Scientists are looking for new antibiotics.

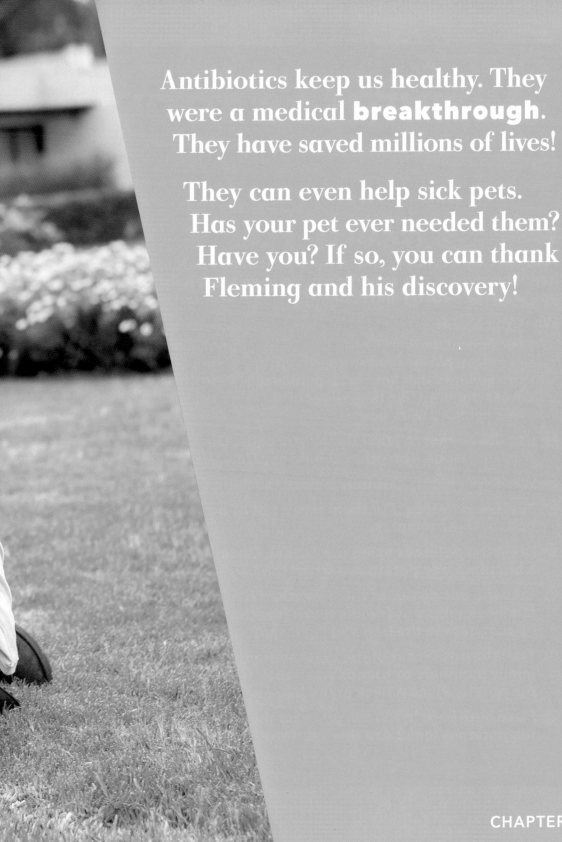

Antibiotics keep us healthy. They were a medical **breakthrough**. They have saved millions of lives!

They can even help sick pets. Has your pet ever needed them? Have you? If so, you can thank Fleming and his discovery!

# ACTIVITIES & TOOLS

## WASHED VS. UNWASHED

Find out why it is important to wash your hands before handling food in this experiment. Have an adult help you with the peeling and cooking.

**What You Need:**

- permanent marker
- two clean plastic food storage bags
- two potatoes that have been parboiled; Waxy potatoes like fingerlings or new potatoes work best.
- vegetable peeler
- pot
- stove
- colander

❶ Use the marker to label the plastic bags. One should say *Washed Hands*. The other should say *Unwashed Hands*.

❷ Wash your hands carefully before touching the potatoes.

❸ Peel the potatoes. Put them into a pot of boiling water and boil for three minutes.

❹ Drain the potatoes using a colander. Once they have cooled a bit, place one potato in each of the bags.

❺ Take the potato out of the *Unwashed Hands* bag. Have a few family members or friends touch it with unwashed hands. Place it back in the bag and zip it shut.

❻ Take the potato out of the *Washed Hands* bag. Have a few family members or friends wash their hands and then touch the potato. Place it back in the bag and zip it shut.

❼ Place both bags in a warm place for three or four days. How do the potatoes look? Are there differences between the two?

# GLOSSARY

**antibiotic:** A medicine that kills or slows the growth of disease-causing microorganisms.

**bacteria:** Single-celled microorganisms that exist everywhere and that can either be useful or harmful.

**breakthrough:** An important discovery or advance in knowledge.

**cells:** Very small parts that make up all living things.

**cured:** Stopped a disease by using medicine or other medical treatments.

**infections:** Diseases produced by germs or parasites living in or on a host.

**mold:** A fuzzy fungus that often grows on the surface of food.

**penicillin:** An antibiotic, produced naturally by particular molds, that is often used against disease-causing bacteria.

**refined:** Removed materials from a substance.

**resistant:** Capable of not being affected by something, such as a medicine.

**vaccines:** Substances usually given by injection to people or animals to protect against diseases.

**viruses:** Tiny agents capable of causing diseases in humans, animals, and plants.

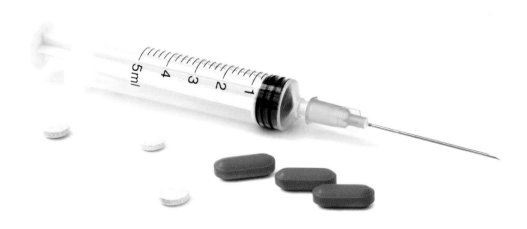

## INDEX

## TO LEARN MORE

Finding more information is as easy as 1, 2, 3.

❶ Go to www.factsurfer.com

❷ Enter "antibiotics" into the search box.

❸ Choose your book to see a list of websites.

FACT SURFER